Discovering Your True Essence

April Sitler

Balboa Press

Balboa Press books may be ordered through booksellers or by contacting:

Balboa Press
A Division of Hay House
1663 Liberty Drive
Bloomington, IN 47403
www.balboapress.com
1 (877) 407-4847

Interior Graphics/Art Credit: Victoria Hawkins

ISBN: 978-1-9822-4300-5 (sc)
ISBN: 978-1-9822-4299-2 (e)

Library of Congress Control Number: 2020902699

Print information available on the last page.

Balboa Press rev. date: 02/21/2020

BALBOA.PRESS
A DIVISION OF HAY HOUSE

ACKNOWLEDGMENTS

I am grateful to all of my Soul Family for guiding me toward the Truth and showing me how to open up my Heart to receive greater awareness of my True Essence.

To be chosen as the vessel for this collaboration with the Creator is an amazing opportunity. I am honored to give these words a voice so that others can remember their True Selves.

I want to extend a special thank you to Victoria Hawkins whose heart and hands created the beautiful illustrations for this book. Her gift of bringing to life the meaning of these words and phrases through color and form is such a blessing for us all.

I appreciate the support of family, friends and Balboa Press for believing in this project and helping make it a reality.

INTRODUCTION

I am so grateful for you and your decision to be reunited with the Truth of YOU!

Life can be difficult. We are surrounded by examples of all that we are NOT that I wanted to create a reminder of who we Truly ARE. This book was created especially for YOU to help you rediscover your True Essence. You are invited to remember that you are very special and precious; your worth and your value are inherent; you are loved infinitely by the Creator. The note you are here to play is so unique that the symphony of life is incomplete without it.

Every page in this book is in the exact order needed to bring about *Your* Healing, Your *Awareness* to the perfection that you ARE! These particular words and illustrations were infused with Light and Love from the Creator to help you reconnect with *your* True Essence and remind you of *your* Purpose and Reason for BEing.

The True meaning can only be *felt* with the Heart. Each time you connect with your Heart and sit with each word, phrase and illustration, you will receive a greater knowing of the Truth that will reconnect you with your True Essence.

I am so excited that you have chosen to make time for you! So find a quiet place and turn each page with the intention that you are going to discover the True You- not the one you have been pretending to be for everyone else up until now. Each time you connect to the guidance offered through these words and illustrations, you will receive a new awareness and even greater blessings.

As part of the journey of finding yourself, let the healing occur at your pace. Sit with each of the pages as long as you need. If emotions arise, let them flow so they can be acknowledged, healed and returned to love. Your Truth will unfold exactly as it is supposed to every time you leaf through the pages of this book. Use the space provided in each section to capture your unique experience in the way that honors you through words, images, and drawings.

I hope that this Divinely guided book helps you discover your True Essence and that you find peace within your Heart.

Now, let the introduction begin . . .

Smile

There is no one else like you.

You are Special!

You are Loved

Live in the Moment.

Just Be.

Listen

You already know the answer.

Trust yourself

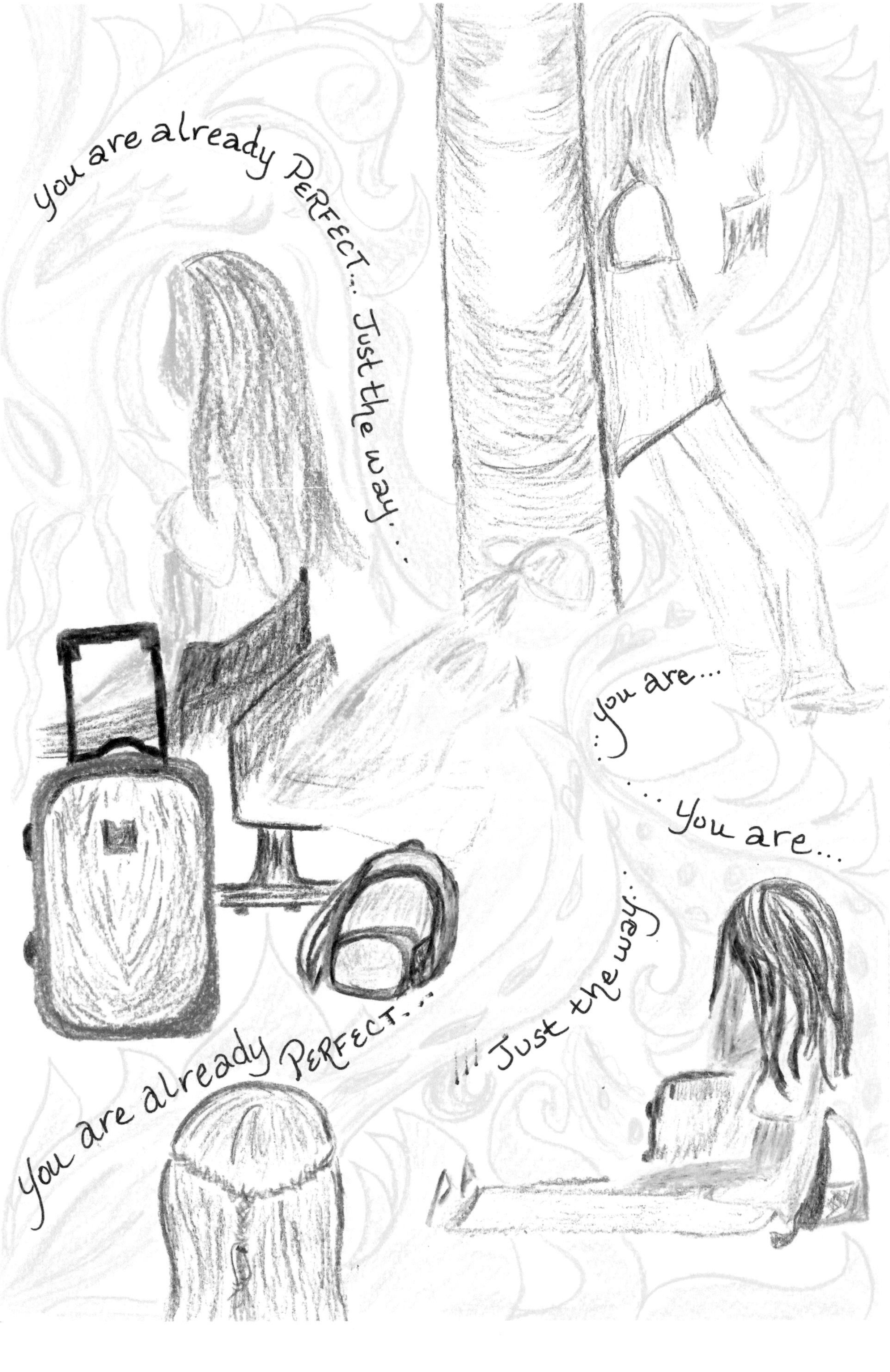

You are already perfect-just the way you are!

~You make a difference~
just Be You...

You make a difference just by being YOU.

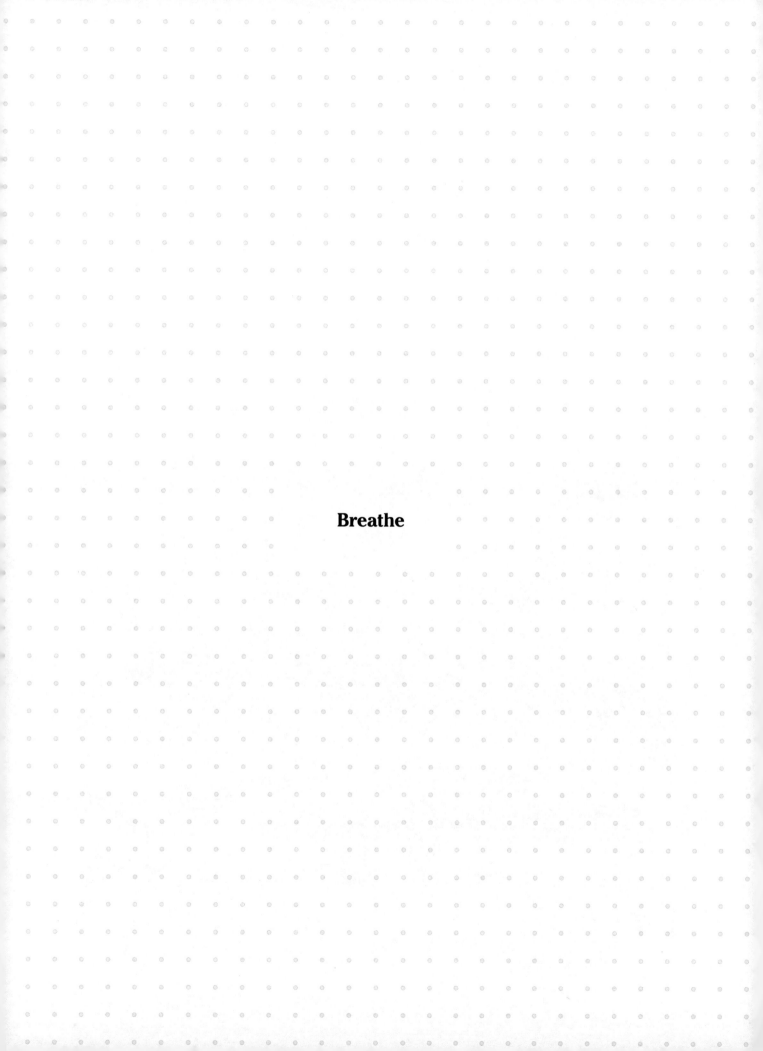

Breathe

You matter to me.

I love you.

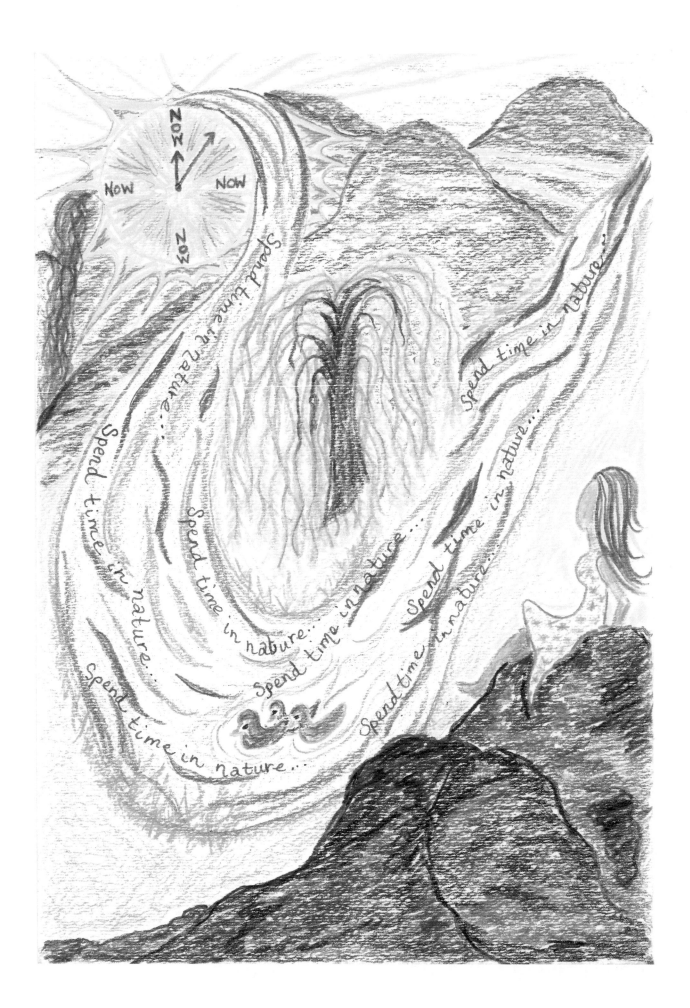

Spend time in Nature
Listen and Receive

Shift your Perspective

Be Spiritually FIT

Share your Gifts with the World.

Live Your Purpose.

Make time for yourself every day.

WHEN
ALL
SEEMS
LOST,
Shhh...
Be
Quiet
And
LISTEN

When all seems lost, SHHHH.

Be Quiet and Listen.

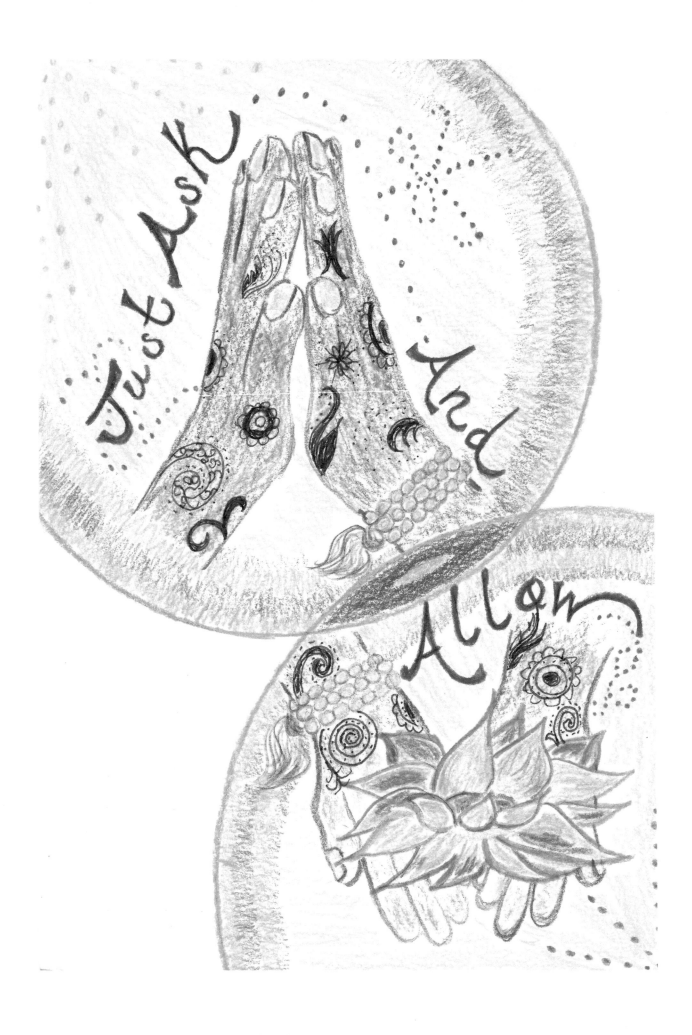

Just Ask and Allow

Life is supposed to be easy.

Simplify

Laugh

Share your JOY with others.

judge less

accept more

Believe in a GOD of LOVE.

Awaken to the TRUTH

Embrace Your Inner Child

Quiet your Mind.

Open your Heart.

Believe in Miracles.

ALL things are possible.

FORGIVE

Share your LOVE

Only LOVE is Real

The TRUTH is in here:

EPILOGUE

Congratulations! You have opened your Heart to Love and Truth. This experience is about connecting your Body and Soul with your True Essence. Rejoice that you have created a space for the Truth to Awaken in your Heart.

Take this journey as many times as you'd like. Your Heart will open to even more Love each time you take a moment to connect with this book.

You are invited to become part of the Discovering Your True Essence community on our Facebook Page where special events and live appearances will be announced. You are also welcome to share your experience with me at DiscoveringYourTrueEssence@gmail.com.

I see you and I love what I see.

May your life continue to be filled with Love and Light!

Many Blessings,
April Sitler

ABOUT THE AUTHOR

April Sitler lives in Texas with her husband and a varying assortment of animals. She is an adventurer at heart and enjoys travelling and experiencing new things. She also spends time in nature a couple of weekends a month at her country home. April loves to create and is usually working on several projects at the same time such as making new items for her Etsy Store, AprilMayCreationsUS, landscaping in her Serenity Garden, scrapbooking, or crafting. April is on a quest to fully remember the Truth, Pursue her Purpose, and Live a Healthy and Vibrant Life.

ABOUT THE ARTIST

Victoria Hawkins, LCSW, E-RYT is an artist, author, psychotherapist, yoga and dance instructor, mom, Suburban Shaman and owner of Hipnique Studio in Tarpon Springs, FL. Victoria has created a Whole Self approach to working with clients of all ages, incorporating art, creative movement, wisdom teachings, yoga and mindfulness. When she creates art for commission or illustration, her desire is to simply be an open conduit of Divine Love to come through. Victoria intends that her art inspires others to remember and experience their wisdom, peace, joy and beauty within.